Songs of the Soul

Jena Oo

BookLeaf Publishing

Presentation by *BookLeaf Publishing*

Web: www.bookleafpub.com

E-mail: info@bookleafpub.com

ISBN: 9789358310269

First edition 2023

I dedicate this book of poems to my family,
A message for them, they'll always have
from me.

I dedicate this book of poems to anyone
who might relate.

To understand you're not alone.

ACKNOWLEDGEMENT

I acknowledge my husband for the encouragement he always gives.

I acknowledge Betsy for sending me the information to achieve this book, and her inspiration when I would occasionally get stuck.

PREFACE

Open your heart and mind. Step into another time. As we walk down this path, forever learning what can last.

Set Me Free

I wish to be free of this dark side
Come back to life with a new light
Tears build up but cannot fall
So overwhelmed under it all
I wish to soar like I used to
Breaking in my wings
Singing to the wind
Nothing like you ever knew
I wish to see the world again
Rising up to take a stand
Defeat the darkness I am left to hide
Fighting off the failures
from the searing world of the other side

All of this may well be true
I am as lost as I am with you
I came down falling
The sky at my feet
Watching the years go by
Slowly coming to my knees
Mighty tears finally fall from my eyes
As lies seem to fly high
Oh what dreams tomorrow bring
Until they come crashing down
I hide my face in the sadness
My wings blackened with sorrow
As I say goodbye for real this time

Little Bean

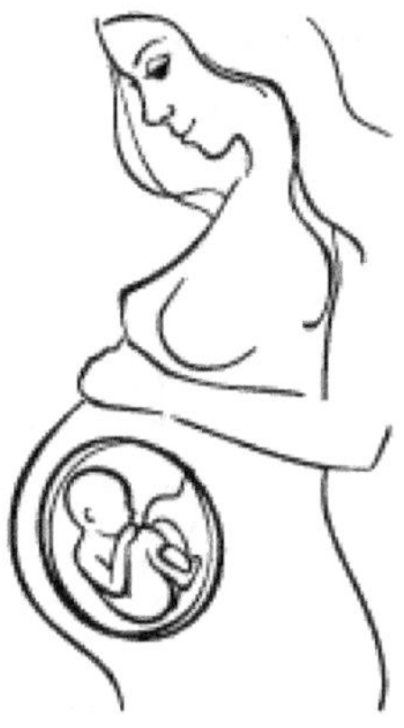

Little flutters begin to grow
As time goes on
More forceful blows
The night is full
Of jolts and kicks
Sleepless nights
And aching hips
The morning comes
With heavy footsteps,
Messy hair,
And swollen legs
Oh but the joy it brings
A new beginning

Learning new things
Though I am torn
Will I be enough
For this growing bean
This journey will be tough
Unlike any other before
But it will be full of love
As a new light is born

Not Alone

It's time to take in stride
The challenges of life
Time to take in pride
The accomplishments
You have achieved
It's time to set aside
Don't let the world
Overrule your emotions
Don't let the dark
Fully rule out your light
Let us stand tall

Through all the doubt
That clouds our minds
Let us scream out
Have the wind
Carry our voices
Someone is there
Someone is here
Stand tall against the allegations
Against evil of any form
Night is dark but not evil
For how is there day without night
Brave your inner demons
Show them who is boss
We are in control
We are the power
We are the light
To a brighter future
Brave the world
As challenges come to be
Time is for you
As it is for me
Need an ear to listen
I am an ear to hear
Come to me
As I can come to you
Let us brave the world together
For you are never alone

Fate Intertwined

It started with a game
A debt to be paid
A card of no value
Starts the strings of fate
One is willing
While the other is not
The distance is unraveling
Scary for a thought
Two separate worlds
Growing closer and closer
As time goes on

The bonds grow stronger
Giving it a try
With nightly chats
Everyday until,
it's time to meet at last
Finally in person
With an everlasting touch
The warmth of the embrace
Chilling and such
Feels like a dream,
A hug from behind
Can it really be true
That you're all mine
Moving forward time
One moves to another
Now and forever
Living together
Tie the knot one year later
By two years' time
Two mini me's have arrived
Hardships fell hard
But we all survived
Coming out stronger
And more Alive
Eight years have come and gone
Today we celebrate
Completing the family
Number three is born
Oh joyous moment

Fate intertwined
In miraculous ways
Our love story
Is like no other
Crazy ups and downs
But the love always stays
Who knew 1 card was all it would take

My Dear

From day one
You were there
Although so far away
I wasn't prepared
To fall in love
And start this story
10 years is a long time
With all its glory,
You have been mine

Though dark times

Have come and gone
Our love stays stronger
Forever on
With you by my side
We can face anything
The light at the end
Of a very dark tunnel
Your voice so angelic
Your touch so warm
Your presence
Energizes my very soul

My dear there is no one
That could compare to you
No one in the world
Who makes me feel complete
The way you do
The family we have created
Tiny humans and furries
Without you in it
The world would be blurry
I'm so thankful we said I do
My dear there is no one else
I'd rather love than you

A Message for Arabelle

My dearest daughter
So feisty and strong
A very caring heart
For everything that's wrong
Your goofy smiles
And rainbow eyes
Make the world better
As time flies by

My beautiful first born
So loving and sweet,

Crazy and loud,
But I wouldn't miss a beat
You're a little monkey
And always getting hurt
I love to hear your stories
And all the energy you exert

My little Arabelle
I hope you never change
From this beautiful strong
Girl that you are
Smart and well-mannered
You are the star
Of your own life
So lead the way
Don't be afraid to be yourself
The silly goofy girl I know
Who loves to play games
And swing on the swings
Who is not afraid
To do anything
Don't let go of that flame
Always spread your wings
Mommy is watching you
Daddy is too
Whether near or far
We are always here to support you
Be a shining star

Home is always here
No matter how old you get
Don't ever let that light disappear
I'm so proud of you
And all you are becoming
Don't ever give up
No matter what
I'll always be your backup
And if I can't make it
Don't you fret
Daddy is always there
You can bet
Baby girl never change for anyone
We love you to the moon and sun

A Message for Julian

My dearest son
So charming and sweet
So caring for others
You don't miss a beat
I love to hear your laughter
And goofy jokes
With you here
Life seems brighter

My handsome second born
Full of energy
And learning spirits
Lover of puzzles
And math equations
Reader of books
You are ready

for any occasion

My little Julian
I hope you never change
From this brilliant little boy
That you are
Ready for anything
You are the star
Of your own life
So lead the way

Don't be afraid to be yourself
No matter what anyone says
You're silly in all the ways
But that's what makes you true
Always have the bright view
You're a little gamer boy
Who loves to challenge himself
Don't let go of that flame
Always spread your wings
Mommy is watching you
Daddy is too
Whether near or far
We are always here to support you
Be a shining star

Home is always here
No matter how old you get
Don't ever let that light disappear

I'm so proud of you
And all you are becoming
Don't ever give up
No matter what
I'll always be your backup
And if I can't make it
Don't you fret
Daddy is there
you can bet
Baby boy never change for anyone
We love you to the moon and sun

A Message for Jayde

My dearest daughter
So little yet feisty
Learning to take big steps
Into this world
Becoming the almighty
Your little giggles
Can cheer anyone up
Dances and wiggles
Are what you love to do
Baby girl always stay true

My beautiful third born
Last but not least
So curious about the world
And how it all can change
I love to watch you explore
And learn what it's about
Although you can be
A little beast
When you don't get your way
You like to sit and pout

My little Jayde
I hope you never change
You know how to stand up for yourself
Don't let others get their way
A very smart little girl
You are the star
Of your own life
So lead the way

Don't be afraid to be yourself
Even if you are shy
Right now you are just turning 1
There's so much to learn
Before we know it
You'll be on the run
Don't let go of that flame
Always spread your wings
Mommy is watching you

Daddy is too
Whether near or far
We are always here to support you
Be a shining star

Home is always here
No matter how old you get
Don't ever let that light disappear
I'm so proud of you
And all you are becoming
Don't ever give up
No matter what
I'll always be your backup
And if I can't make it
Don't you fret
Daddy is there
you can bet
Baby girl never change for anyone
We love you to the moon and sun

Moonlit Song

I'm calling out for a rescue
Can anyone hear my voice
I'm calling out for a rescue
Find the path to me

I'm sitting here in the darkness
Will you be my saviour
I'm sitting here in the darkness
Shine your light upon me

I must not leave this place
As I am bound by thee
Can you share your world today
And help to set me free

The water is my home
But sometimes it's so cold
Can you come and warm me up
Before I get too old

I'm calling out for a rescue
Can anyone hear my voice
I'm calling out for a rescue
Find the path to me

I'm sitting here in the darkness
Will you be my saviour
I'm sitting here in the darkness
Shine your light upon me

The moon is bright tonight
So full and beautiful
Come watch with me
Here in this tunnel

I'll lead you to a waterfall
With an underwater cave
Lots of secrets beneath it all
That you cannot escape

I'm calling out for a rescue
Can anyone hear my voice
I'm calling out for a rescue
Find the path to me

I'm sitting here in the darkness
Will you be my saviour
I'm sitting here in the darkness
Shine your light upon me

The Dark

The world feels dark around me
It closes in every night
I can feel its grip around my neck
As I turn out the light

I shutter in silence
As the voices sing their song
I'm just trying to find
The place where I belong

I cry deep inside
As I curl into a ball
I really want to live
I try to give it my all

But sometimes it's not enough
I always seem to fail
They just don't see who I can be
How can I prevail

The world feels dark around me
It closes in every night
I can feel its grip around my neck
As I turn out the light

Endless War

War is everywhere
No matter what you do
People scream and fight
There is nothing new

Blood stains the ground
Bringing up beautiful roses
Bodies falling down
Becoming the earth's food

Endless years of war
Everywhere we turn
When will it end
Can everyone just learn

Learn to be kind
Learn to care
Learn to see people
For who they really are
Not just someone to dare

If only we could stop
And see the truth behind
Everyone's own self
Their thoughts and their mind
No matter where they are from
If they're short or they're tall
If only we could see
Underneath it all

We could learn about each other
Open our hearts and mind
Share our cultures openly
The similarities you might find

But alas it's too difficult
For these feeble minds
To understand to share not take
Instead of being blind

Fear

What is this feeling
That makes me tremble
Shudder at the thought
Makes me nimble

What is this sensation
That gives me goosebumps
Makes me want to hide
In a hole or a trunk

Something that is taught

We are not born with it
We use it as a tactic
To harm and to hit

This simple emotion
Can cause a world of trouble
This thing we learn
Makes you want to form a bubble

Trembling
Shaking
Hiding
Faking

Running fast
Like the earth is quaking

Fear
An everlasting emotion
Fear
Trembling sensation
Fear
Something that is taught
Fear
An uncontrollable rot

Forever More

It's your time now
To spread those wings
I wish you the best of luck
On your path to freedom
Freedom from pain,
From suffering and sorrow
I'll be here remembering
All the good times we had
Forever in my heart
Will your footsteps stand
Thank you for your teachings

Thank you for your love
Life will be hard without you
But I know you're up above
It's time to say goodbye
To your physical form
I'll still see you in my dreams
Forever more
I know when I need to talk to you
To tell you my stories
I just close my eyes
And feel your energy
You will say don't worry
Don't wait around for me
I'll be okay
Go where you need to be
I'll see you again one day

Dear Best friend

You are so far away
My day is your night
But our love doesn't waver
Even when we fight
We talk when we can
And have each other's back
Don't forget
I'm your biggest fan
I may not be there in person
But you can tell me your stories
I love your progression
Of who you want to be
I'm so proud of you
And all you are becoming

Even if we don't talk
For months at a time
We pick it right back up
You'll always be mine
To be honest
We have never really fought
We may disagree
But it's not a lot
I'll always be here for you
Through thick or thin
You are like my man
And I am like yours
That's why you are my best friend
Till the day we die,
forever more
But even then,
That's not the end
Till our souls
Don't exist
The strings of fate
Will bring us together
Time and time again

Writer's Block

I want to write
The stories flow in my head
When I take my pen
It all just disappears

So I sit and think
As the time ticks on by
It just won't come back
Even if I try

Inspiration can come and go

At the drop of a dime
Can't be forced
Have to let it flow
Otherwise it's wasted time

Writer's block
Is real and true
Sometimes you just
Don't know what to do

Don't keep it locked away
All the emotions you carry
Let it free
With your energy
But sometimes it's not enough
And you simply just feel stuck

Little Baby

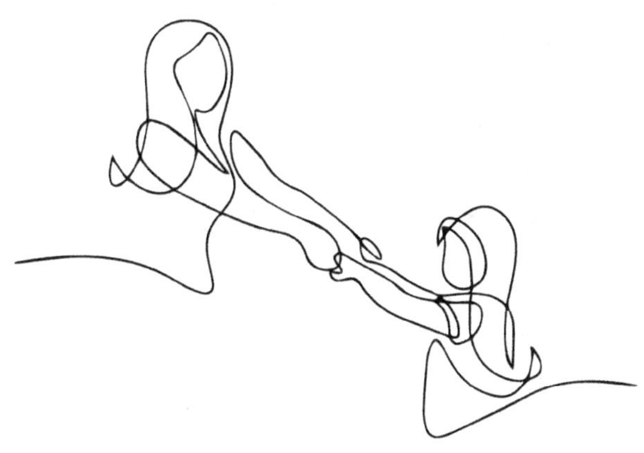

I try to feed you
But you cry
I try to rock you
Yet you cry
When I put you down
You start to scream and shout
Baby, what is it about

Mommy is trying here
I don't know what you want
I know you are tired
But you fight it hard
Your diaper is dry
Your clothes are fresh
Not too hot or cold
You just need to rest

Go to sleep
My little baby
Dream a dream
My little baby
Close your eyes
And rest your head
And dream a dream
A happy dream instead
Mommy is here
So don't worry
Mommy is here
My little baby

I'll hold you close
Right here in my arms
Where it's safe and warm
For as long as you want

Go to sleep
My little baby
Dream a dream
My little baby
Close your eyes
And rest your head
And dream a dream
A happy dream instead

A World of Evil

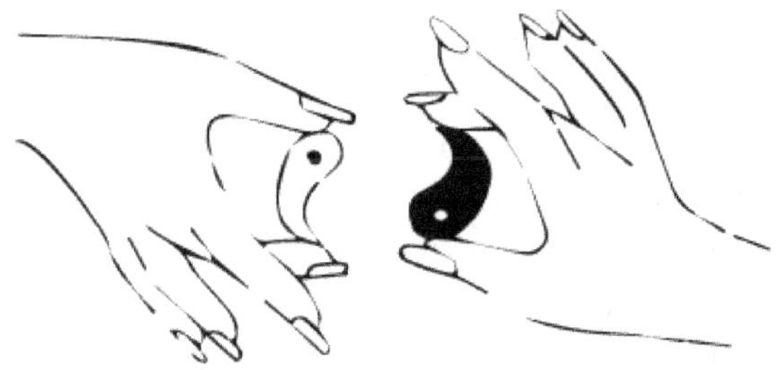

Banish from this world
The hatred and sorrow
Violence around
Every corner

Banish from this world
The blindness people see
Oh the greater things
Everything could be

Banish from this world

The greed people feel
The hurt that they do
To get what they want
Is all too real

Banish from this world
The evil in thy hearts
That makes murder seem
Like a fun time to plot

Banish from this world
The corruption of men
Always get what they want
No matter how thin
The world is full of dark
Worse as time moves on
Though Yin and Yang are one
Yang is changing
Without darkness there can be no light
Without light there can be no darkness
This may well be true
But if darkness takes over
Everyone will be blue

Meowtastic

Soft and furry
Feisty yet sweet
Their soft little sounds
Make you warm inside
A nice little treat

Pink little toe beans
Rough little tongue
Some may be cuddly
While others are done

Purr purr purr
A sound so lovely
These simple vibrations
Make a beautiful melody

Chasing a ball
Or a tiny red light
Zig zag across the floor
Oh what a sight

Then it's time to sleep
Most of the day
Just to have zoomies
When the moon comes to play
Soft and furry
Nice and warm
Meows so majestic
Without a worry

What makes a kitty
So full of personality
To fill the day
With warmth and love
You'll never be gray

Don't Look Back

He comes in the night
Creeping in the shadows
Oh what a fright
Don't look back

Keep a straight face
Don't show fear
For if you do
He will be near

Stay away from doors
Stay away from windows
He's been here before
Don't look back

Creepy sounds he makes
To try and trick you
Calling your name
It can't be true

If you feel that he's close
Be brave my friend
Everyone now knows
Don't look back

Out of Time

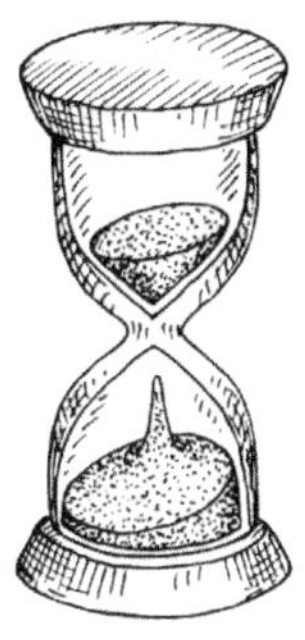

Rush rush rush
No time to spare
Gotta go fast
The deadline is here

Crazy frenzied hair
Bags under eyes
Oh goodness the time
Just before my demise

Can I make it
Or will I not
Time is ticking
On that clock

Think think think
What can I do
Eat and drink
And sit down too

Oh I got it
The brainstorm has hit
Oh sweet relief
No time to quit

Time

Time is precious
We can't get it back
Live and love life
Gotta pick up the slack

Before we know it
In the blink of an eye
Our babies are bigger
Running their own lives

Our pets become older
As we too age
Time is precious
At any stage

No time to fear
To sit and cry
I can't do it
Before you even try

Take advantage of freedom
Do things you love
Spend time with loved ones
Get out and be active

Time is precious
To just sit and waste away
Make your own story
Start your adventure today

www.ingramcontent.com/pod-product-compliance
Lightning Source LLC
LaVergne TN
LVHW041236200726
843507LV00013B/2713